Thundering Landslides

Heinemann Library
Chicago, Illinois

Louise and Richard Spilsbury

Designed by David Poole and Paul Myerscough
Illustrations by Geoff Ward
Originated by Dot Gradations Limited
Printed in China by WKT

07 06
10 9 8 7 6 5 4 3

Library of Congress Cataloging-in-Publication Data
Spilsbury, Louise.
   Thundering landslides / Louise and Richard Spilsbury.
      v. cm. -- (Awesome forces of nature)
Includes bibliographical references and index.
Contents: What is a landslide? -- What causes landslides? -- Case study:
Aberfan, Wales 1966 -- Where do landslides happen? -- What happens in a
landslide? -- Case study: Sarno, Italy 1998 -- Who helps after a
landslide? -- Case study: Nepal 2002 -- Can landslides be predicted? --
Can people prepare for landslides? -- Case study: San Gabriel Mountains,
California -- Can landslides be prevented? -- Crushing landslides of the
past.
   ISBN 1-4034-4786-1 (lib. bdg.) -- ISBN 1-4034-5444-2 (pbk.)
   1. Landslides--Juvenile literature. [1. Landslides.] I. Spilsbury,
Richard. II. Title.
   QE599.A2S75 2003
   551.3'07--dc21
                                          2003011622

Acknowledgments
The author and publisher are grateful to the following for permission to reproduce copyright
material:
Cover photograph by Sipa Press/Rex Features.
pp.4, 10 Sipa Press/Rex Features; pp.5, 6, 23 Jean Miele/Corbis; p.7 Daniel Dancer/Still
Pictures; p.8 Carl Orlandi/AP; p.9 Crown/National Assembly Photo Unit; p.11 Jun
Dumaguing/AP; p.12 Damian Dovarganes/AP; p.13 Georg Koechler/AP; p.14 Stefano
Cardini/AP; p.15 Maxim Marmur/AP; p.16 Plinio Lepri/AP; p.17 Franco Castano/AP; p.18 Zhu
Wenjie/AP; p.19 Arno Balzarini/AFP; p.20 Devendra M. Singh/Getty News and Sport; p.21
Binod Joshi/AP; p.22 U.S.G.S; p.24 S. Grant/Trip; p.25 Getty News and Sport; p.26 R.l.
Schuster/U.S.G.S.; p.27 Los Angeles County Department of Public Works, Alhambra,
California; p.28 FTX/Rex Features.

Some words are shown in bold, **like this.** You can find out what
they mean by looking in the glossary.

Contents

What Is a Landslide?

When large amounts of rock, soil, or mud slide down a hill or mountain, it is called a landslide. Landslides can change Earth's surface very rapidly. They often happen without any warning. A mass of rock, soil, and mud tumbling down a steep slope is heavy enough to destroy anything in its path. The force of a landslide can knock over houses and other buildings. When large amounts of mud slide down a hill, they can bury whole villages below.

Landslides often pick up other things as they move. A landslide can move trees, cars, trucks, animals, and people. The damage caused by a landslide can be made even worse when it carries things with it.

Within just a few minutes, this landslide claimed the lives of hundreds of people in a village in El Salvador.

Different kinds of landslides

Landslides can have different names. **Rockfalls** happen when big chunks of rock break off steep mountainsides or cliffs and fall to the ground below. **Rock slides** happen when chunks of rock slide down a slope. **Mudflows** happen when wet soil or **debris** flows downhill as a river of mud.

Landslides come in many different sizes. A rockfall may be just one boulder or it could be millions of tons of rock. Landslides also happen at different speeds. Soil can slip down shallow slopes at just a few feet each year, but some mudflows travel faster than a speeding car.

LANDSLIDE FACTS

! Landslides can travel at over 260 feet (80 meters) per second.

! Around the world, landslides injure or kill hundreds of thousands of people each year.

This landslide took place above the Indus River in Pakistan. Tons of earth and rock poured into the river below.

What Causes Landslides?

If you put an eraser on a flat ruler, it will not move. If you tilt the ruler, the eraser eventually starts to slide. In the same way, rocks and soil can begin to slide if a mountain or hill is too steep.

Steeper slopes

Mountainsides and hillsides can become steeper naturally, often because of **erosion.** Erosion is the wearing away of soil or rock. Erosion can be caused by rivers, waves, wind, or rain. Slopes often become steeper if the land changes shape during an **earthquake.**

Slopes can also become steeper because of things people do. When miners search for useful rocks and minerals such as coal, they often pile up soil. This creates new, steeper slopes of land that can slide downhill.

When people build roads through mountains, they sometimes cut through the mountainside and create steeper slopes.

Changing slopes

Landslides are also more likely to start if a mountain or hill changes. Mountainsides naturally change over time as pieces of rock break off, or as soil dries and crumbles. These changes create more loose **debris** on the surface. After a **volcano** has erupted, it may leave a new, heavy coating of loose ash on the mountainsides around it.

People also change hillsides. When they build houses and other buildings on slopes, this adds extra weight. The extra weight can cause the soil and rock underneath to slide more easily. People also affect hillsides by cutting down trees. The roots of trees and other plants on mountainsides help hold the soil together. Without plants to hold the soil in place, it can slide more easily.

Landslides are more likely to happen on bare slopes where trees have been cut down.

What starts a landslide?

Landslides are started by many different things. The most common **trigger** is water. Soil, rock, ash, and other **debris** change when they get wet. They get heavier as water soaks into them. As they get heavier, they become more likely to slide downhill. Water is more likely to trigger a landslide if a lot of it arrives at once. Heavy rainstorms, **floods,** and warm weather that melts snow suddenly can bring a lot of water.

In some parts of the world, **earthquakes** trigger landslides. Earthquakes can shake mountains and hills so much that the rock and soil on them starts to slide. Sometimes loud thunder can also cause landslides. People can start landslides accidentally. For example, people sometimes use explosives to make highway or train tunnels through hillsides. The blasts cause **vibrations** that can start a landslide.

This flooding mountain stream in Italy is washing soil and rock onto the road, making it dangerous for cars to pass.

United Kingdom, 1966

Aberfan is a village in the United Kingdom. For 50 years owners of nearby coal mines piled up waste from the mines on hills above the village. At 9:15 A.M. on October 21, 1966, thousands of tons of black **sludge** suddenly slid down toward the village. Heavy rains, which made the sludge very wet and heavy, triggered this landslide. The sludge buried twenty houses and the local elementary school.

> "It was a tremendous rumbling sound. Everyone just froze in their seats. I just managed to get up. I reached the end of my desk when the sound got louder and nearer, until I could see the black out of the window."
> Gaynor Minett, a student survivor

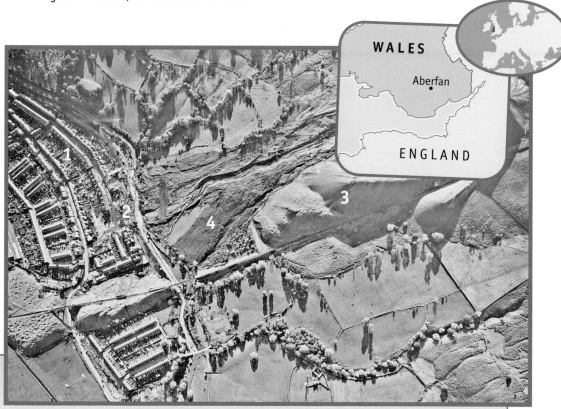

This aerial photograph was taken shortly after the Aberfan landslide. Marked on the photograph are: 1) the village; 2) the school; 3) the coal waste; and 4) the landslide.

Where Do Landslides Happen?

Landslides usually happen where there are steep mountains or hills. The most dangerous landslides often happen at the edges of large mountain ranges such as the Himalayas in Asia, the Rocky Mountains in the United States, and the Andes in South America. Some mountain areas are more likely to have landslides because they have many **gorges.**

Landslides also happen along coastlines with steep cliffs. Strong waves **erode** the bottoms of the cliffs. The erosion causes rocks and soil to fall down from above.

Earthquake and volcano areas

Landslides are also common where there are **earthquakes** and **volcanoes.** Earthquakes and volcanoes often **trigger** landslides. Earthquakes and volcanoes are common along the western coasts of North and South America, in Japan, and in southeastern Europe.

Winter storm waves usually cause the worst erosion along coasts.

Landslide seasons

Landslides can happen at any time of the year, but they are much more common during wet seasons. In **tropical** parts of the world such as Central America, summer is the wettest part of the year. The rain makes soil much heavier and rocks more slippery.

In **temperate** places such as North America, the wettest and coldest weather occurs in winter and spring. Rainwater seeps into the cracks in rocks. When this water expands, it can break the rocks into pieces. These pieces add to the loose **debris** that can become part of a landslide.

This landslide took place in the Philippines in July 2002. It was triggered by a week of heavy rains.

LANDSLIDE ⚡ FACTS

! Many landslides in the United States happen on slopes that have been cleared of trees.

! Each year landslide damage in the United States costs around two billion dollars.

11

What Happens in a Landslide?

Landslides often happen without any warning. However, sometimes there are signs that a landslide is going to occur. When soil and rock begin to move before a landslide, the movement may crack water and **sewage** pipes in towns and villages. Water may bubble to the surface or damp ground may appear in places that were dry before.

There may be other signs in buildings and streets. New cracks and bulges in streets can appear. Concrete patios and telephone poles may start to tilt. Buildings can twist, causing windows and doors to stick.

The next disaster

Sometimes landslides happen after other natural **disasters** such as **earthquakes** or **floods.** These landslides can make things worse for people suffering from damage caused by the first disaster.

Sometimes there are no warning signs that a landslide is coming. This 1989 landslide above the Mexican village of Acalama killed all but 30 inhabitants.

During a landslide

When a big landslide moves down a slope, it can destroy everything in its path. Landslides shift tons of rock and soil. Moving rocks bang into other rocks and make them move, too. Pieces of rock can act like rolling marbles, making larger pieces of rock slide more easily. As the landslide moves, it grows in size, pushing along more and more trees, rocks, and other **debris.**

Tons of moving rocks can crush buildings, people, and vehicles. **Mudflows** enter and surround buildings. As it dries out, the mud can become as hard as concrete. Landslides can knock down **power lines** that may injure or kill people by **electrocution.** Landslides can also break oil and gas pipes. Leaking oil and gas can easily catch fire.

Mudflows fill spaces around buildings and cars. This can make it very difficult to rescue people who have become trapped.

After a landslide

Even small landslides can shift the ground under buildings, causing them to collapse. Even if a building remains standing, it may not be safe. Landslides can damage a building's foundation. The building may collapse without warning later on. People are also affected when landslides **contaminate** water supplies. When water pipes are damaged, dirt gets inside. If people drink contaminated water, they may catch diseases.

Landslides can block or break roads, railways, and bridges. This makes it difficult or impossible for people to travel. When roads are damaged, it is also more difficult for rescue workers to reach landslide victims. If falling **debris** damages telephone lines, people may not be able to call for help.

Blocked roads like this one can slow down rescue work after a major landslide.

Can landslides cause other natural disasters?

Landslides can cause other natural **disasters.** One natural disaster that can be caused by a landslide is **flooding.** If mud and rock fall into a river, they can make the water flow up over the sides of the river. This is the same thing that happens when you get into a full bath. When something is added to the bathtub, the water level rises. When water flows out of a river and onto land, it can flood towns and villages and ruin farmers' fields.

If a landslide splashes into water in a **fjord** or harbor, it can start a giant wave. This type of wave is called a **tsunami.** In 1934 a landslide in a fjord in Norway started a tsunami that killed hundreds of people.

This 2002 flood in northern Afghanistan was caused by a landslide that blocked a river. More than 100 people were killed.

Italy, 1998

The small town of Sarno sits at the bottom of a hill in southwestern Italy. Scientists had warned people that the area was unsafe to build on. It was unsafe because the soil on the hillside was at risk of sliding. The causes for this risk were clear. Some of the hillsides had been cleared of trees to make space for buildings. Others had been stripped bare by forest fires. In the town many houses had been built too close to rivers. They could be **flooded** easily if water levels rose.

In May 1998 strong rains **triggered** a massive **mudflow.** Mud and **debris** shot through the narrow streets of Sarno. When mud flowed into the river, it caused flooding. The river water made the mud thinner, so it flowed even faster. Within a few minutes, the mudflow had ripped apart buildings and bridges.

"The force [of the mudflow] is incredible. It crushed cars as if they were [soda] cans." Jim McConnell, a construction **engineer**

The mudflow in Sarno devastated the entire town.

Mud everywhere

The mud flowed into every part of the town. At a local hospital, the mud came through the windows and doors, and it knocked away part of the staircase. Cars and ambulances were piled on top of each other. In other areas, roads and train tracks were covered in piles of debris and boulders that had been carried by the mud.

Many people were washed away or buried by the mudflow. Roberto Robustelli was rescued after being trapped in a space 1.5 feet (45 centimeters) high and 3 feet (1 meter) square. He remembered:

"At first I thought, 'Oh, I can make it, I can make it. There is enough space to breathe.' But the time kept passing and I started losing hope."

Over 130 people died and hundreds more were injured or left homeless by the **disaster.** Several thousand people could not work or go to school for weeks.

Who Helps After a Landslide?

People caught in landslides need urgent help from others. For example, people trapped in buildings or under **debris** need to be rescued quickly. Other help is needed during the weeks and months after a landslide.

Firefighters and police officers rescue people who are trapped and take them to safety. Ambulances and medical workers arrive as quickly as possible. They treat people who are injured and take anyone who is seriously hurt to the hospital. Workers and **volunteers** for **aid organizations** such as the Red Cross also provide help. They set up **shelters** for rescued people. They also give food and drink to the victims and rescue workers.

*Rescue workers often risk being caught in **floods** or further landslides while they work to rescue or treat people. This man is being dug out of setting mud after a 2002 landslide in Shenzhen, China.*

Military helicopters may bring things that people need. They can carry in all kinds of things, from tanks of clean drinking water to heavy lifting equipment for clearing debris. They can also fly injured people to the hospital if roads have been cut off.

Long term

Later, workers clean up rocks, mud, and debris. **Engineers** check buildings to make sure they are safe. Some buildings may need to be rebuilt. Roads, bridges, drains, fences, and **power lines** may need to be fixed or replaced.

Sickness after a landslide

People's health may be affected for some time after landslides. For example, a **virus** that is transported on dust causes a disease known as valley fever. Many people caught this disease after a 1994 **earthquake** in California. The earthquake had **triggered** landslides that threw huge amounts of dust into the air.

After a 2002 landslide in Switzerland, workers helped clean up the huge amounts of debris.

Nepal, 2002

In the summer of 2002, heavy **tropical** storms and **floods triggered** landslides in different parts of Nepal. Many of the landslides happened in remote mountain villages that could only be reached on foot or by helicopter. But it was not safe for helicopters to fly because of bad weather. Also, Nepalese emergency services did not have enough workers or equipment to reach all of the landslide sites.

The Nepal Red Cross was one of the first **aid organizations** to help the landslide victims. The organization had emergency supplies and a large number of local, trained **volunteers.** The volunteers had to walk a long way to the villages affected by landslides.

"Volunteers made it possible for the Red Cross to work with the community immediately after the **disaster.** Red Cross volunteers have walked for five days to assist remote communities." Bob McKerrow of the Red Cross

These people in Nepal are clearing mud from the area where houses were swept away by the 2002 landslide.

Getting supplies

The volunteers helped rescue trapped people and treated victims who had minor injuries. Nepalese police and soldiers organized flights to take supplies to the affected villages. At one place 32 families came to collect supplies.

Nima Sherpa's family and their herd of cattle survived one of the landslides. But they were left without **shelter** against the cold mountain weather. Sherpa had never asked for help before. "It is so embarrassing to ask for help," he said. Sherpa received supplies that helped his family live through the difficult times until they could rebuild their home.

These Red Cross workers are preparing supplies for people left homeless by the 2002 landslides in Nepal. A typical rescue kit might contain items such as cooking equipment, clothes, candles, blankets, and tablets that make water clean enough to drink.

Can Landslides Be Predicted?

Predicting landslides is not easy. **Geologists** use a lot of different information to figure out whether rock and soil on a hill or mountain might slide. Then they know if a landslide might be **triggered** by certain weather, such as heavy rain.

Know your slope

Geologists examine places where previous landslides happened. Landslides may happen in those same places in the future. They study the cracks in rock. Rocks with cracks might break up more easily than rocks without cracks.

Scientists also use cameras on **satellites** to take pictures of Earth. These pictures allow scientists to study remote places. Scientists look for hillsides and mountainsides that have few plants and trees on them. Landslides are more likely to happen on bare slopes than on slopes covered with trees.

In addition to photographs from satellites, geologists use handheld equipment to study the angles of hillsides and mountainsides.

Spotting changes

Geologists pay special attention to hillsides and mountainsides in places where many people live. They check these slopes regularly to see if they are changing. Geologists compare satellite pictures to see if the slopes are getting steeper.

Geologists also test to see if the soil and rock is getting wetter. They look at weather forecasts to see how much rain or snow will fall. This extra water may trigger landslides. They also use special equipment to detect ground movements. These movements can show when an **earthquake** or **volcanic** eruption is about to happen. These natural **disasters** can trigger landslides.

Making things worse

Prediction becomes more difficult when people change the land. For example, when people drain land around a river to build houses, the river often **floods** more easily. Flooding can weaken the bottom parts of hills and mountains. The slopes above can slide more easily.

Geologists use powerful computers like this one to predict landslides.

Can People Prepare for Landslides?

In some areas landslides are a constant threat. People who live in these areas can prepare in different ways.

One way is to make slopes more stable. To stop **rockfalls,** strong walls can be built at the bottom of a slope. These walls are made of concrete blocks or wire cages filled with rocks. Tough wire netting can also be attached to the slope. The netting prevents rocks from falling, or it controls where the rocks fall. People also plant trees on slopes to stop the soil from moving. In some places people build strong concrete walls or channels. These structures direct a landslide away from towns.

This road in Laguna Beach, California, is protected from landslides by tough wire netting.

Another way to prepare for landslides is by building carefully. For example, if people use **flexible** water and gas pipes, the ground movement during a landslide is less likely to break them. Thus, the risk of **flooding** and fires after a landslide may be reduced.

Emergency plans

In areas that could be affected by landslides, people should know what to do. They should learn **evacuation** routes. For example, people should know how to get to the nearest high ground. They should know never to try to outrun a landslide. Families should also plan where to meet if a landslide happens when family members are in different places.

*People in potential **disaster** areas should keep an emergency pack like the ones being prepared here. These packs often contain a battery-operated radio so people can hear information about the landslide. They also might contain a flashlight, food, and clean water.*

San Gabriel Mountains, California

The city of Los Angeles, California, is built at the base of the San Gabriel Mountains. These mountains lie on the San Andreas **Fault.** A fault is a giant crack underground. The two sides of this fault push against each other and force the rock on top upward. This means the San Gabriel Mountains are getting higher. As they get higher, many of the mountains are getting steeper. Steeper slopes mean more landslides. As the rocks move, they also make cracks under dams and in pipes. When water spills out of these cracks, it makes the soil and rock even more likely to slide.

This photo shows the damage caused by a 1995 landslide in the town of La Conchita, California. About twelve homes were either destroyed or badly damaged.

Making Los Angeles safer

Engineers in Los Angeles are trying to prevent landslides in the future. They are building **debris** basins. These basins are shallow pits shaped like football stadiums. They are built in places where landslides may happen. When a landslide happens, the basins catch much of the rock, soil, and other debris.

There are over 100 debris basins around Los Angeles. So far these basins have caught over 20 million tons of rock, soil, and debris that have slid down from the San Gabriel Mountains. When a basin fills, construction workers use power shovels and trucks to empty them. Emptying the basins is expensive, though. It costs over 60 million dollars per year to do this.

Here, construction workers are cleaning out a debris basin north of Los Angeles.

Can Landslides Be Prevented?

People cannot prevent all landslides. The only sure way for people to avoid landslides is to live far away from mountainsides or hillsides. However, this is not always possible. Many landslides start because of natural causes such as **earthquakes** or heavy rain. Nothing can be done about these causes.

People can prevent some landslides by being more careful about the way they use the land. For example, they should allow trees to grow on hillsides. People can also make some future landslides less damaging by studying steep slopes around the world. If people understand more about landslides, they may may be able to prevent them in the future.

A village like this should be safe from landslides. The mountain behind it is covered with thick trees that can help prevent landslides.

Thundering Landslides of the Recent Past

1966, Rio de Janeiro, Brazil

Heavy rains caused landslides on the mountains near the city of Rio de Janeiro. They killed around 1,000 people.

1971, Chungar, Peru

A landslide fell into Lake Yanahuani. It caused a huge wave that crashed into the nearby town of Chungar. The wave killed more than 200 people.

1974, Huancavelica Province, Peru

A landslide blocked a river. The river **flooded,** creating a huge lake. The landslide killed over 400 people, and thousands had to **evacuate.**

1980, India

Heavy rains set off landslides in the Himalayan Mountains that killed 250 people.

1981, Sichuan Province, China

Heavy rains **triggered** landslides that killed 240 people and left 100,000 people without homes.

1985, Colombia

When the **volcano** Nevado del Ruíz erupted, it caused a **mudflow** that killed over 20,000 people.

1990, Iran

An earthquake caused mudflows that buried whole towns and villages.

Glossary

aid organization   group of people who work together to raise money and provide help for people in need

contaminate   poison or harm the water, land, or air

debris   broken pieces of buildings, trees, rocks, etc.

disaster   event that causes damage and suffering

earthquake   shaking of the ground caused by large movements inside Earth

electrocution   when someone is killed or injured by electricity

engineer   person who plans or designs

erode (erosion)   wear away by wind, rain, water, or rubbing

evacuate (evacuation)   move away from danger until it is safe to return

fault   place where two or more plates meet below Earth's crust

fjord   narrow strip of sea between high cliffs

flexible   can be bent or twisted

flood   large area of water covers land that is normally dry

geologist   scientist who studies rocks and the way Earth's rocks were formed

gorge   steep-sided river valley

mudflow   flow of wet soil and debris downhill as a river of mud

power line   cable that carries electricity

rock slide   tumbling of rocks down the side of a hill or mountain

rockfall   pieces of rock break off a steep mountain or cliff and fall to the ground below

satellite   object made by humans and put into space. Satellites do jobs such as sending out television signals or taking photographs.

sewage   waste matter from toilets and drains carried in sewers

shelter   safe place

sludge   soft, muddy waste material such as that created by coal mines

temperate   warm and dry in summer and wet and cold in winter

trigger   set off or start

tropical   area near the equator that is hot all year round

tsunami   huge wave created by an earthquake or landslide

vibration   shaking back and forth

virus   tiny living thing that can cause diseases

volcano   opening in Earth's surface through which lava, hot gases, smoke, and ash escape

volunteer   person who offers help without being paid

More Books to Read

Jennings, Terry. *Landslides and Avalanches*. North
  Mankato, Minn.: Thameside Press, 1999.

Newson, Joyce E. *Natural Disasters*. Milwaukee:
  Gareth Stevens, 2002.

Suen, Anastasia. *The Red Cross*. New York: Rosen
  Publishing Group, 2001.

Index